The Girl with a Thousand Eyes

Feminist YA Poetry

by

JI STRANGEWAY

GYATRi MEDIA   Los Angeles

THE GIRL WITH A THOUSAND EYES

Copyright © 2017 Ji Strangeway. All rights reserved.

No part of this book may be reproduced or transmitted without written permission of the publisher or author.

Cover Design: Liga Velina, www.ligavelina.com

Published in 2017 by GYATRi MEDIA, Los Angeles

Publisher's Cataloging-in-Publication data

Names: Strangeway, Ji, author.
Title: The Girl with a thousand eyes : feminist YA poetry / by Ji Strangeway.
Description: Includes index. | Los Angeles, CA: GYATRi MEDIA, 2017.
Identifiers: ISBN 9780998877815 | LCCN 2017907427
Subjects: LCSH Strangeway, Ji. | Poetry, American. | Feminist poetry. | Women--Poetry. | Young adult poetry, American. | Lesbians--Poetry. | BISAC YOUNG ADULT FICTION / Poetry | YOUNG ADULT NONFICTION / Poetry
Classification: LCC PS3619 .T741 G57 2017 | DDC 811.008--dc23

DEDICATION

Youth are told spirituality doesn't come until they get old. Orthodoxy tries to convince us that spirituality and sexuality should be divided. Feminine Wisdom knows otherwise. This book is dedicated to Her thousand eyes.

POEMS

WE ARE ALL DONKEYS   1
TWENTY   2
VANISH   3
BEFORE HER   5
BROOKLYN IN RAIN   6
UNTIL DEATH DOTH SHE PART   8
BROKEN   9
IN DEPENDENCE   12
SKIN   14
BLUE WOMAN   16
CRUEL PLEASURE   18
AMERICA KILLS   19
THE END'S EMBRACE   21
REALITY OF RAIN   25

II

BROOKLYN   31
MY SACRÉ COEUR   32
JUST ONE BLISS   33
THE SALT AND THE SEA   34
MORE THAN MYSELF   38
SUFFERER   41
OBSIDIAN   42
EVEN IN PLAIN SIGHT   44
THE CHINESE HERBAL EYE DOCTOR   47
SOME THINGS DON'T CHANGE   49
THE UGLY ONE   50
THE OLD GREAT DONKEY   52

III

ON DEATH 57
IN THE BEGINNING 59
LIKE RAIN 60
AND I 62
THE GIRL WITH A THOUSAND EYES 63
SCRIPTURE 2:22 64
SAME HOUSE 66
YESTERDAY 71
YES 72
THE TRUTH ABOUT NOTHING 74
FORMIDABLE DIGRESSION 76
THE MUD IN ME 78
THE HATE POEMS 81

AUTHOR BIO 83
TAGS 85
FOLLOW 87

PART 1

WE ARE ALL DONKEYS

We are all donkeys
grazing the same grass.

The bulldozer roars
louder than the driver.

The driver
is taller than the farmer.

The farmer
is taller than the grass,

but the grass is greater than all…

and we all graze

on the same grass.

TWENTY

I love you like a blind man
touching your body for the first time
knowing your beauty by form
loving the indescribable.

I love you in this blindness
of my ignorance to see
the one I most deserve,
because the hole in my heart
leaves me always empty.

I picture the Grand Canyon
without end to her depth.
Rivers that once rushed through
groped every wall of her body,
loved her so completely
never to think it would leave
a barren masterpiece.

This infinite emptiness I feel
is the void many travel to see,
yet can never touch
the bedrock of its being.

I cannot recognize your vastness,
yet I've mapped you out
like the whole of Arizona.

I love you with perceptivity
of a blind man feeling the difference
between one dollar and twenty.

And you are my twenty.

VANISH

the encapsulation of my new york life
moth light
inside the cage of time tacking
me against four corners of the calendar
prison light
those subway rides in and out of clubs
disco light
injected with boys' cologne

time with its pulse on my wrist
go-go girls drunk and high on e
masturbating on the everest of amplifiers
climbing shadows
pray to the maze
filling my mind with bass

spin the cube on astor place
skate punks from suburbs fake
begging for alms from other poor artists
blowing last dimes on starbucks

years of east village dwelling
idols buried in tompkins square
trying too hard to be unique
to be creative
to be more than we are

sidewalks outlive selfish pride
no one dies before their time
a girl once treated me like ghost
but then she vanished

only these words live

i will not cling
to everything
it must be like lint
to me.

BEFORE HER

For the girl I did not meet
held stitches before our eyes
hidden behind world sewn wonder
extract the heavens upon your smile.

For the girl I did not meet
did not pronounce your name three times
remembered your eyes a thousand times
and masturbated once in your image.

For the girl I did not meet
stood alone and incomplete
summoned by strangers and lookers-on
dare to meet you, to compete.

For the girl I did not meet
left as fractions on the street
chase heart-blown kisses we have missed
think of you as days and years delete.

BROOKLYN IN RAIN

Above the pharmacy,
night dark and moist,
cars rush along housing projects.

Brooklyn would never be the same.

Above the pharmacy,
above the G-train
on Classon & Lafayette,
homeboys roam the streets...
her bedroom window appears dark from outside.

But from within this room... the sign reads clearly:
"Pharmacy"... red letters on white...

I can see each face within each car passing by... unconcerned.
I breathe upon the window...
traces of her hair, golden, dripped with shadows.
Thick, hot breath brushes my neck...
"You want me to fuck you... you're so wet," she says...

Souped-up cars rev at the corner red light... her fingers press
tightly in-between... then dig deeper... the green says "go"
... for the thrust.

I'm on all fours, pushing backwards and forwards... as traffic
rushes side to side...
we all meet and collide like strangers, never touching... sharing
subconscious experiences.

Above the pharmacy,
no one sees these faces making love in public spaces...
yet, something feels

especially romantic
about Brooklyn in rain.

I think... G-train... g-spot, it's all the same.

For lo, the winter is past, the rain is over and gone
- The Song of Solomon

UNTIL DEATH DOTH SHE PART

She, voluptuous—
nice round tits brush my lips
as I extend my tongue to warm the
cool wetness, she could devour if
not breathing so heavily—
in spite of fingers tight
inside her grip,
with feet and toes
riding my back
spreading her ass…
She, with her eyes—
looks down to see
how the red bulb glistens
like pomegranate as its
fear of whites undress
strip with my teeth.
I slurp in the Breath of Life,
which she can't take
as we contemplate
exactly about
how Conservative she is,
without her rhythm and swinging tits
fall forth and push
to suppress mine.
And this fantasy prevails
in due time,
as all reality is lost
to the Mercury of Love.

BROKEN

You are the architect this time.

When the angels walked away from my heart,

you followed them out.

Where did they take you?

Some place far away…

to a distant land.

In Israel, you go with the angels.

You take their hand.

My eyes, do you miss,

or the way I count your beauty marks?

When the sun eclipsed,

you followed the rays…

where does this burning heart take you?

Back to the desert…

some place warm,

where life bakes with all those who wear your face.

But I'm not the one who changed.

I stand still.

You mistook my shadow for the truth,

robbed G*d from my heart.

I have never walked away from you

when I feared, I didn't run.

When I knew I couldn't love you—I became a hunter

I learned to smell tracks

I became a scuba diver

I learned to extract pearls.

My fingers, do you miss

the ones that point inside?

I never once thought I was such a bad design.

But you are the architect this time.

My life, I do miss.

It was something I lived with you.

And now that you are no longer here,

I remain nowhere…

My soul rests the same.

I recline.

Dear girl, your heart is searching

for something you had already found.

You have the tools but not the skills.

Build as you may

a dollhouse of useless dreams.

They are made of thread

and when they break, you'll then be

in the same place,

right where I am,

so broken.

IN DEPENDENCE

Night, if She calls, tell her I'm not here.
Tell her I'm not living with the lonesome ones.
Night, if She comes, tell her I'm not here.
Tell her I am not holding my heart tonight—
night, tonight, to Her, to night—
my breath has become silent of your voice.
Night, O night, ignite
cracked fireworks; score your body into meaning, to night.
And night, tonight—
they watch you with starry eyes.
They watch you, family, child, lovers, and clutching enemies
hold tight.
What have they done to you
on the 4th of July?
… without me?
… as I have been stood up
and up
and up, and up, tonight.
Everyone witnesses your smooth skin tearing open,
but I—
hear your birth from a distance,
as stabs of light bring you
to cum.
I have witnessed,
even with closed eyes
how the after-rain wind
cools my skin,
clouds spark blue,
confusing the difference between
lightning, death, and the life bursting unto you.
They could never reach you

if they tried...
but at least
they try.

SKIN

Skin
The same identity worn since birth.
I baked within the oven of my mother and—
skin.
The outfits at discount stores can't cheapen you
and
skin.
Never slashed, never half off… yet
priceless—
skin.
Skin
shaved as my head, my pussy, my armpit—
never naked enough to be skin, as the meaning of skin.
My cat wouldn't know it,
yet she has skin.
Skin
stained on such things
as life challenges, near-death, and certain warm liquids
men and women, girls and boys would spill onto me,
only to forget,
not knowing my skin or myself of theirs.
Skin
shedding off life and death like snakes…
not noticing what pieces of me left along the way
and which have stayed.
Skin
unlike memory,
unlike soul,
unlike love,
unlike, and not liked, and liked,
more fragile than light, which peels off the surface of each day.
And I call to you,
Skin
for your warmth, your nakedness,

and the texture, which I can't feel nor possess,
and I ache within the thing I wear that looks so much like yours,
but yours is better and newer because
yours is worn by everything… and I am not everything.
Skin
you are that which makes my soul mates,
as siblings, as neighbors, as partners, as enemies, as lovers, as friends.
No one knows you, yet cling onto you
upon their last breath.
Skin
I am absent of you, yet covered by you
you who are an exception to rules
of life and death.
In old age, I will be dropping my suit,
but Skin,
I would still wear you.

For Anne Sexton

BLUE WOMAN

They stuck you in a century
like an insect under glass…
a chemical vaporizing beneath the male beaker—
you—
dense and thick…
Woman.
Forest… they could not handle you
cradled you within
the arms of social waste:
get married… make babies
and eat antidepressants on the hour
by the hour
at the hour
in the hour…
and how I've died the way you lived… and lived the way you
died,
and how I've never wanted to be pinned like you—
and how so many today become you…
goddess undercooked—baking for millennia
in a gas oven literature calls History.
But you were never His…
and never a part of his story.
Too woman for woman
and too woman for words,
I live for your maker,
and break the vein that bound you
to the world-class class classic classy classicism…
entitled
………………...American Life.
Convention has made you dull
you are my bold knuckles
G*d-given truth.

Nothing could turn you blue…
neither asphyxiation…. mood pills
nor Death.

CRUEL PLEASURE

mourning the death of my weak self
i watch people live their allotted life
each life, a forsaken treasure held to highest esteem
only for youth to be whittled away by time's cruel pleasure.
earth is nothing more than a mortuary
cataloging bones and bodies;
each makes claims to nobility, fame, or simplicity
to fade into nothing more than memory.
each cycle of life, we become one another
forgetting the purpose and reason for why we came,
wishing to make a dent on personal affairs
wishing to dominate those affairs on others.
this civilization is artwork colored in stencil;
when the hoary find their way home to the creator
their hands molded by time are rendered useless.
had they asked even once—what truly made their hands
they would have lived forever.

AMERICA KILLS

Mary was not his mother.
Virgin was not her breast.

Hands, darkly supple
holding suspended breath.

His eyes are life as grave.
His grave is wide as life.

His skin, both child, yet worn, like seastone,
my father, a soul who ran from home.

I called to mountains west.
The sun fainted slowly into night.

I called to the mountains east.
The moon smiled yellow and bright.

I called to the sea of south.
Monks left leaves bitten to dust.

I called to the sky of north,
angels flocked with fright.

I called within and found my father.
His face was blue like a rock dipped in somber.
The world suddenly collapsed like a weak lung
as my father wept emotions

he had never felt before.

I have but a long, fast journey,
arriving at the soul that spat three-quarters of his blood
adjacent to my heart.

I find a life that left him narrow,
turned him blind,
blindly turned him,
turned he blind.

This is a song about sadness,
a melody of remorse,
a hoarse voice hollow,
an immigrant's discourse.

America grey almighty,
Star-spangled nothingness.

You have stolen the man who wore Beauty
and made him refugee.

Remember Eddie Adams
as he shot America's face white,
white face at night,
night worn with American white.

Remember his picture as a picture of father,
father of all fathers.

When my father was shot,
America killed itself.

THE END'S EMBRACE

Once I held my heart
upside down.

My memories tread
deeper
lower
reversing
the cycle of my life.

I have never had this experience
before
yet
I bathed in it
inside my mother's womb.

When I arrived
into this life
I came out
upside down.

My heart
was upside down
my belly
was upside down
my breath
held in reverse
elongated inside
the palms of my being
as if breathing too soon
would destroy
all of my
reality.

I held my breath
for my mother
for my creator
for my universe
for my society
and what they would make of me.

I held myself
preciously
for the world
and the mysteries
of my beginnings
in that breath.

One thousand turmoils
wound tight like a spinning top
could throw the most devout
into a head-on collision
with the G*dhead itself,

but nothing
no roller coaster
natural disaster
world tragedies
could ever
turn you

upside down

like birth

like that place

where you first became

something

resembling

the reality

of the Heart

itself.

At the end of this life,

non-reality will carry my breath.

Until then,

my breath is held

for the father, whose face I have not kissed

for the child I did not bear

for the lovers I did not wed

for shortcomings prolonged by guilt.

Non-reality holds this for me

and once again

I will be upside down

for the End's embrace

make no mistake...

She receives us all with a smile

on Her face.

THE REALITY OF RAIN

In the big suburban house
lives a man and a woman.
Their kids have all left home.

Upon return,
father has cancer
mother working alone.

Around the block,
the supermarket is bleak
and dead.

I buy groceries
to feed the family
that once fed me.

I have flashbacks of my life
growing up in
shopping centers.

The garage door opens.
I enter into the family mall,
where all Life
is artificially pure.

I feel
unsafe in this replicated house,
but safe
within my own belonging.

So many rooms
inside this house
lead to nowhere…

Four bedrooms
three baths
yet
this man and woman
share the utility room
next to the garage.

I venture through
many unused rooms,
yet there is no room.

My mom and dad
obsessed with time
have clocks strung everywhere:

on top of the TV
suctioned onto the bathroom mirror
propped up beside exit doors
embalmed in the trinity of picture frames.

There is so much time
in this house,
so many malls.

I had hijacked a thin blue blanket
from the plane back to Denver
claimed it as my meditation robe
and took a flight back home
within this home.

Wrapping the cloth around my frame
I closed my eyes to begin my descent.

I'm not going anywhere.
I don't belong anywhere.

As I traveled

my ears became windows
and I could perceive everything
from miles away.

The impossible happened.
I heard the rain before it came
I had heard the rain.

PART 2

BROOKLYN

As I walk up the stairs,
I walk up memory.
Although the steps are silent—
they speak.
At the door—
she wore a little girl's face—
her lips, stitch, broke.
Oh sweetness,
did you see
how when we kissed,
Love rolled down my face?

MY SACRÉ COEUR

I've known you before
a perfect girl with perfect laughter
darkened by hard knocks of reality.

I've seen you before
immaculate wisdom splitting down center—
love's breastbone.

I swim inside
the delicate pools of your mind
paled by the moon's spastic kiss.

I hold you
like a secret parting her lips
only through G*d's wish.

I shiver in the cold breath
of night flashed with light.

I became a thief of time
as I stole eternity
from you eyes.

Soul spread Her wings
upon your inhalation
you caught my awe—

love gasped,
your eyes lifted
opening
and closing
the sacré coeur.

JUST ONE BLISS

On the day of the last goodbye,
I burst inside with flames of suffering.

Tears, hot like boiling rivers, sped from my eyes.

My lover strokes my back,
her hands beat like waves parting...
leaving me.

In walks the Girl with the Thousand Eyes.
She didn't want to see me cry...

"You shed your soul for the wrong things.
Cry only for the strength of your heart
to love in greatness."

I became naked to the witness's
secret.

Messenger,
one day
I will follow you home to the G*d
from whence you came.

THE SALT AND THE SEA

rosh hashanah,
those things new york.
I thought we could be friends
so fled with you, with the jews.

we piled into my jetta
got lost
near jfk.
through dance beats,
the night struck my
heart
just as strong
as we were
no longer
girlfriends.

I thought we could be friends.

I thought we could be friends
at the table
filled with women
with strange names
like "boots"
and "candy"
who were mistresses
of the yemenite throwing
the party, while
his wife stared bitterly
across the linen clothed table,
scarfing down
her pride
and cancer.

I thought we could be friends,
sitting through
hours of rituals
of wine and slicing
holy bread.

"may it be your will,
lord our g*d and g*d
of our ancestors"

you interrupted
to tell everyone
how thrilled
you were about moving back
to israel.

all is holy
except us.

the zions toasted the
sweet new year
and wished you well
as I swallowed tears.

no one knew
that, with your words,
you had stabbed me
twice
three times
over
and over
again.

I tried to hide
from the pain
that we were only friends

friends sleeping together
for five years
friends that shared your
cancer at 23-years-old,
and I never
left your side.

I dismissed myself
to the backyard
where staten island waters
touched the dark belly
of new york city.

and I stared out at
the statue of liberty
across what has become
the dead sea calling
freedom
freedom
freedom

her torch
obscured by
windless flags
star of david
and red, white, and blue
flanking the yemenite's
yacht.

the salt of my tears
was in the atlantic
as I tasted
you leaving me.
and I asked,
who is the exile now?

for I am the
real jew,
this asian girl
transfused with you,
who loved you more
than ancestors
pocketing red cells of
your own
blood
and for what purpose?
to avoid loving idols
that shouldn't
be worshipped?

yet, I
resisted
g*d
sliding
down
my cheeks,
and tasted
sorrow
parting
my lips
as though
they were
that great,
great
sea.

MORE THAN MYSELF

When we were born
eyes gazed inward,
our first kiss
was birth itself.

Days to follow
with earth's feet warm,
clouds muscled forward
for a storm.

When I arrived,
you had a feast baking
two souls preparing
just right.

I used to lament,
perhaps, cried in sleep
fearing loss
for the moment of this life.

Whenever I left
your face lingered
behind half-door
waiting for the kiss
of our gaze.

I would have wanted
nothing else.
I wanted
nothing less.
Any more was just too much.

We were
just right.

But married couples
weld too nicely
cannot remember
the love that singed us
together forever.

I lay on my belly
to remember this birth
I sit on my head
to press the stars back home
I dream on my side
to let our life sift like sand-clock.

On certain days
she would declare,
"You don't love me anymore.
I can feel it!"

Are you genius, I wonder?
Telepathic?

I search for you again
my love, my life
a winter that has passed.

It's not that I no longer love
perhaps, mourn the loss of love in memory
the time that captured us like butterflies
that couldn't spill their colors if they tried.

Perhaps, I slept too deeply
did not awaken to you
but only to wanting more.

Perhaps, I dream of too many faces,

looking for those thousand eyes
lingering
behind half-doors.

Perhaps, I cannot say goodbye
to the magic and mystery of birth.

We have both lost
our creativity.
It is G*d's gift.

Re-gifting is a sinister thing.
I would not give your love
to someone else.

Wondrous girl
I love you among all the rest
nothing short of
nothing tall.

It is just right.

But in my heart, I love the world
more than I love myself.

SUFFERER

My tears are hot

cool, not like sweat

nothing like water

not like the rain.

My tears are warm

come from the heart

maker of love

the blood of beginnings.

When I cry,

cry, not from my eyes

but from my sight

eyes of the heart…

Knower of Love.

OBSIDIAN

nights sweating humidly
snuck in easily
like that.

i'm racing in my car to meet no one
and the sex i thought i had with others
was really with myself.

music trickles like metal rain
hot bass thumps iron nails
into my dead self

fashionistas stick to disco lights
like moth
morning
comes
like men (too soon)

i missed
i missed the moon.

the toast is cold
but soothing with exhaustion
red vinyl seats of a brooklyn diner

my fears hidden
in others' glum expressions

i thought i was larger than life
yet the coffee sludge was more alive

i remember park slope
because i lived and died there

with the ugly wealth so
filthy rich—that they were fecal rich

they don't give a shit.

i slept in my office
with my calico cat
listening to dark rhythms
of tribal house beats

i throbbed with the pulsation of a life
(i thought i knew)

i had no worries
because my life was a lie.

i did everything
to skip sunlight
and blew all my earnings on nocturnal
vip rooms bathroom walls
bent over sinks, finger fucking
undressing...

i had everything,
yet my life was so meaningless

i don't understand why she waited for me
to live hard and with all my might

and when i lost it all,

she opened her palms
to give me the sun:

the vanity of darkness
in the heart of an obsidian.

EVEN IN PLAIN SIGHT

Six in the morning,
Chinatown, New York is no other than Bangkok
the barren streets are a storm that just left town
the people of Chinatown are pellets of rain
when they arrive, everything gets drenched.

Street cleaning trucks wheel by—
steel hairbrushes spin for the sake of sound.
I think, Why bother? Chinatown stinks always,
with or without garbage.

This is the smell of Bangkok, but chilled with
Winter's Grin.

Morning, photographic gray
Nobody changes here
Nobody stays
Chinatown fingerprints our lives
day by day.

You don't need to be Asian
you can mark your entire life
by the Zodiac of Chinatown.

My lover and I played Centipede at the arcade
we closed the photo booth curtains
spun the seat and timed our faces
we tried to save the day.

JFK Jr. lived nearby…
he drowned quite far away

even if Gandhi swung by,
nobody stays.

When the World Twin Brothers fell
just elbow distance away,
Chinatown's countenance held still
no death lingered on her face.

This town is a selfie always in itself.

Invisible artists shop at Pearl Paint
Invisible actors bring fame to anything they eat
Invisible politicians shake hands with shopkeepers
Invisible tourists gawk at suicide ducks on display.

I am one of the invisibles
Chinatown's reality, never real
she's a mother who doesn't embrace
"Tough love," they say.

No merchandise charms, "I (Heart) Chinatown"
Unabashed city,
it's just your feng shui.

My friend just moved to Bayaud Street
(the Trump strip among the Red)
at her rooftop, Life is painted metal:
silver surrounds us like a black & white photo.

"Look," she said, "There's a Chinese flag."

The dusty shred flung with incognizance

True to form, half-glanced from above and below.

Nobody can see this flag
even in plain sight.

Its eyes look not to my eyes.

I salute

all life

gone by.

THE CHINESE HERBAL EYE DOCTOR

Chinatown,
the doctor opened wide
saw matching blood shots
floating like sail-less boats.

The edges of two worlds
paired on my face... dim.
Shake it like a light bulb
to check for that jingle of death.

The room smelled like dying saints,
like soundless sounds of plants
when their cell ponds evacuate.

Does the broccoli scream when we eat it
the way a giant eats a tree?

Answer:
See the tree, not when it falls.
The soundless sound is Ignorance itself.

You just asked yourself
if you were stupid.

Under the watermelon vein,
he checks for tears.

Points to black stars
scattered on twin round skies.

"You eat too much meat," he says.

I replied,

"Perhaps we kill too many vegetables."

He closes the map and sends me home.

My eyes, a map
of health,
of habits,
of happiness.

He didn't tell me anything
I didn't need to know.

These eyes,
the road back home.

SOME THINGS DON'T CHANGE

Columbus Park in Chinatown
New York City has never been warmer than dust.

Chinese children run and frown,
old men blink like turtles.

Ten years ago, I crossed this path,
where toddlers with bowl haircuts flop.

It doesn't cease to amaze me
how time has stopped,

because ten years ago,
kids who were once ten
are now twenty,

and the memory still holds my footprints.

THE UGLY ONE

in my past life, i was a caterpillar.
i sponged to thick, flat green leaves,
clung to them and siphoned laziness.
i wanted to do nothing but sleep.

i was a fat and ugly one,
brownish-black with matted fuzz.
i lived like an idling rusting junk car,
but i loved living.

i loved to stick to things.
i curled under the backside of leaves.
i would slide upside down to show off
how good i was at not letting go.

the best times were when the tropical
raindrops pattered my skin.
they were fat and lazy as me.
i felt enormous encouragement when
i was doused.

it glorified how wonderful it was
to slumber through life.

because i was so ugly,
nothing wanted to eat me.
others must have thought that i tasted
as bad as i looked.

but now, all this is in the past.

i remember now.

i remember how i loved
to hold onto things.

THE OLD GREAT DONKEY

Feelings deeper than water

my mind has forgotten
but the heart remembers

spring winds wet with wonder
eternity weaves roots at my feet

days darkened by puberty
reality ripped like torn sheets

my mother's face when she was thirty
her aged happiness at sixty

my father's brazen self-suppression
his heart carried like water balloon

my own fate trembles
salt releases from the sea
dust pounds from a pillow

I walk on rickety memories
a plank of loss
with honeycomb feet

facing life
a coin that flips
death half smiles
like Mona Lisa

no greater or less than…

less than death,

greater than life,
greater than death,
less than life.

Our allotted life
flipped like a coin.

Which side is greater?
always half
in-between
jagged lines
drawn by childhood
driven by adulthood
slaved by ambition;
as we all become
that old great donkey
returning to the farm
to die
just like Robert Bresson's
Au Hasard....

au hasard... old great Balthazar!

greater than life,
greater than death,
less than life.

Our allotted life
flipped like a coin.

Which side is greater?
always half
in-between
jagged lines
drawn by childhood
driven by adulthood
slaved by ambition;
as we all become
that old great donkey
returning to the farm
to die
just like Robert Bresson's
Au Hasard….

au hasard… old great Balthazar!

PART 3

ON DEATH

There's no tragedy on her face.
Death takes you like the child life offered.

We bring to death all sorrows of loss
but in dying, we are martyrs –
a star shining its brightest
though faint to the naked eye.

Death receives you, upside down
just like the mother
just like Life.

It does not judge you
It does not expect anything more or less
It takes everyone
It embraces.

Death has not darkness.
It has not light.

In the womb, all is darkness,
yet we are fearless.

When the light poured through,
we were born mixed
with the fluids of our mother
and that of illusion.

The mother we held
never leaves us at death,
for Death is a mother
who takes us all
in any direction
without asking

as violently as birth
as gently as womb.

When someone dies
we cry
just like we did
when Reality streamed into our eyes.

IN THE BEGINNING

When the sky turns blue, infinity falls.
You say it's a shooting star—
but it's just words, my love.
In the beginning, there was the Word
and it broke into pieces.

I taste G*d in the beginning
until the silence is overtaken
words you'd never think to say,
promises that leave you cursing.

She waited on the arms of the bridge,
like a dreamer lounging on a crescent moon
her eyes atypical of the guardians
shaped like triangles.

In Vermont, she had a girlfriend
a new one for each year
(and I would be the third).
"If you smoke," she said, "Do it on the porch.
My mom hates it, even though she died of lung cancer."

I told her I would never go
to the country house that might hear us fucking
when she bathed naked in the pond
I didn't want her mother's ghost
to see me dipping into her daughter
floating on her back.

I find her on the third chapter,
tasting life without salt
gobbling words of affection and nonsense
soup of illegible alphabet letters
making stipulations that leave us guessing...
whatever happened to silence?

LIKE RAIN

Weakness, it is all there
but time won't let us down.

The distance ahead
is hurried and tangled.

But ours is the strange way
like a river in motion
waves rolling in all directions
for the sake of one destination.

You lead me this way.

Sea green,
those two dots that mark
pinpoints of your eyes
they are anchors of gravity
and I'd be lost without them.

Slender,
your body a labyrinth
with unconventional peace
I make home of solace
in not reaching
your embrace
knowing
your breath is the door
that will lead me through.

I come to you
unexpected like rain.

The intro is loud

until I glide down your skin
silent as the eyes
of doves...

Let me kiss you
so eternity can pave
the way.

AND I

Morning rise
the sum of stars, like unorganized soldiers
line up to die...

The sun, like a brutal mother
kisses each baby star on the forehead—
and swallows them up.

We lay naked side by side,
coddle our dreams in separate worlds,
sugar pours upon our stirring thoughts—
coating everything we can't forgive...
hardening them for survival.

To awake within each other's arms—
your breath melts upon my eyes,
your kiss, like the morning star—
swallows me whole.

I am made anew each time.

Again and again we meet, join, die...
your face changes from sunset to sunrise
yet, it is always the same sun that is met with each day.

I say, "This is what it means to live and die."

And you... and I.

THE GIRL WITH A THOUSAND EYES

The thousand eyes
spare no soul
save no one
know everyone
live a dazed consequence
yet alert and direct.
She shares the universe
with just one breath.

SCRIPTURE 2:22

For this moment I knew

your glance no longer further to mine

your lips fold a secret

you could no longer look into my eyes.

For this moment I knew

although you said I was no longer "the one"

I knew that your heart doth lie

when your inverted glare cradled only truth.

For this moment I knew

our love was not an artifact

made of cheesy love songs and half-heart bracelets…

I could feel our lives pressing closer as we tried to say goodbye.

The never-ending truth is that love shall not leave us

with tears filling up the pockets of our cells,

I sweat your beauty

I breathe through your breath

I look through the world with your eyes

and I could never deny

that for this moment I knew—

within the downward drift

of our human demise—

we have buried the most sacred truth:

this bible of our lives.

SAME HOUSE

Same house
same gray
same sky
same

newly planted trees
newly planted ducks in
newly dug lakes
leaving nothing
to the hands of nature.

Arvada, Westminster, Colorado
wherever you are
here you are

Suburbs.

Same view of blocks of time
sitting on top of the next
as I walk this block,
it is new, yet same.

Not once
would I ever have imagined
finding comfort
in this artificial kibbutz.

Not once in my life,
yet this time
I let my soul mesh
with all things
cold
all things
concrete.

For years, I've slept
behind black walls,
staring out at the yellow bus
these kids that board—all hate me,
because I am not fake
like them.

When we arrive
at the fake school
I pick up fake pens
read fake books
eat fake food
and fall in love with
deeply fake girls.

On days, tormented,
I'd say goodbye to Mom
and walk to school
yet never arrive.

I'd hide behind
tall red-brown cedar fences
wishing my life would end.

At night, I stared out from
double-paned windows up at the moon
trying to see through eyes
through glass
through clouds
through night
through moon to see the Real
but it didn't come
and I thought
it never would.

I slept with demons,
entering the orifice of my soul
only they knew
they knew what was real.

When Time, with its precise
cold knife cut me from pubescent life
I walked the new earth
and headed east.

I returned as an adult
to my aging parents'
melted White life.

6 am
I walked to the fake pond with Mom
she talked about her pains
her knee
my father's surgery
exercise
health plans.

I listened the way
I never had before.

She did two rounds
of her oasis
as I surrendered to one.

Walking back home
I closed my mind's eye
and stared deeply into this
prosaic life: endless opening
to neatly trimmed gray paths
concrete, yet not concrete,
not real

and then
the Vultures came.

Oh, dear Suburbia,
you've eaten nearly

half of my life.

The eyes of same-houses
wrapped with synthetic evergreens
hinged at my blind spots
stared back at me.

This time
I let everything consume me
I walked the sidewalk of death
as cement planks bend wide
drowned by sprinklers shedding
their blank souls overshooting the grass.

Vultures circled
but could not find me.

When the pavement curved further away
I followed the distance only to return
to the same place

Same-house
same-rosebushes
same-parking
same-stillness.

I looked at cookie-cutter windows
and their never-ending demise
and saw for the first time:
"This pretty house couldn't be ours."

It looked like one of those homes
you wish you lived in.

Same-house
same-life…

But now, there is this new

Reality.

YESTERDAY

Today, my grandmother observed her own bags
the muted yellowish camel tone with spots comfortably snug
deep as the Sun takes its seat.

Today, she pulled at the drawstrings… noticing how Time closes
the pouch nearer.

Across the bag that transports her bones, like a balloon half-filled
with water, the stitches cling to dead cells rising up for air.

She tests the durability of her assigned wardrobe by plucking
away, letting me give it a go…

I pull up a tentful of finger-pouch and watch its disregard sling
back.

The feel of old age is nothing like any tangy fruit leather or
perplexed silk swimming with immortality.

It is that, a bag of stitches stretching at the seams, crisscrossing
with traffic heading towards and away from breath.

It feels like just that, "my old skin" she says, observing it as if it
behaved badly just yesterday.

YES

Yes is beautiful
more than you know
more than your
eyes
lips
crevices
beneath
those
hips.

Yes is
more than words
honey
love
vows
opening
precious
gifts.

Yes is
newness
light
gold
sun
first
kiss.

Yes is what I say
when you long to know
with dire want
admittance
utmost
trust

as if
this were
your
one
and
only
breath.

THE TRUTH ABOUT NOTHING

The donkey saw today

how you behaved,

and said nothing.

The donkey got kicked today,

and said nothing.

He drank from the stream

and saw the heavens

crowd around his ears,

but said nothing.

Slaves passed by him for centuries

for he too, is a slave.

In the donkey's eyes

he sees his past life:

in the past, he was a donkey

in the present, he is a donkey

in the future, he remains a donkey.

How did his life persist unchanged?

Did he defy the laws of karma?

Of heaven and hell?

He is a donkey,

because we are all donkeys.

This truth will never change.

When you realize that you are

who you are,

you too

will say nothing.

For Kathleen

FORMIDABLE DIGRESSION

To dream of the sequence.
Scrounged to the floor
                      in which our categorical selves lay
like naked bones—
                      become extinct to our beginning
                      tho' never buried completely.

To implore
beneath soil
                      or completely hidden from place—
your heart, a treasure I have
found—
                      buried too quickly now, again
                      this rare stone
to which birds have mourned
and sung songs
like this before
to meet with life, their casual greeting,
and be with life their wings.

For you, I carry my wings
as witness to
                      who you are...
a spectator coming to participate—
indulge in the Being we hope for.

With this
                      another tune,
circle of songs turn and cross corners...

I've come to this life, this sky,
to explore—

                       two birds as one...

one less,

                                    one more.

For my beloved, Kata

THE MUD IN ME

in the traffic
of your presence
i lose direction.
a silent rush nears me
building anticipation.

it is possible
you have always been with me
timeless like fruit on a tree:
though dies by the season, for eons
always bears the same shape.

it is possible
you will see me in my old age
and find me back here again
somehow
in some place
remembering the same letter
i write today
that i have probably
written countless times before
to lovers
secretly speaking
your name.

it is possible
for all i have lost and won
none of it means anything
like a cheap ticket
to a vegas show.

with all the entertainment life offers,

i rest the jewel of my mind
on the pillow of your divine.

in dreams, i have fallen in love
ten thousand times
with the most radiant stars
each rendezvous leaves me stunned
like a tree of life
struck by insight
impressed
and nullified.

it isn't until i remember
to love with nothingness
that i become fit to dissolve
like sand in rain.

i know not where nature
takes me or how i would
be shaped again.

if i were to become mud
you will silence
and reduce me
to nothing
be nothing
never again to
pretend.

from my useless body
i grow many things
that remind me
of you.

the delicate surrender
of a seed to its mother

from this, i turn
into a beautiful flower.

although the mud in me
cannot see

this is how i love,
for you and i have been
and shall always be.

THE HATE POEMS

The Hate poems
are never as good
as the Love poems.

ABOUT THE POET

Ji Strangeway is a film director, author and poet based in Los Angeles. She is the creator of the female-centric, coming-of-age film, *Nune* and YA graphic novel *Red as Blue*. Writing from the margins of gender, orientation and circumstance, Strangeway's work is an unconventional call to action. Her words are for the dreamers and idealists.

TAGS

Aging, 49, 52, 66, 71, 78. *See* Time
America, 16, 19
Beauty, 2, 19, 64, 72
Breath, 6, 8, 12, 19, 21, 32, 60, 62, 63, 64, 71, 72
Brooklyn. *See* New York
Chinatown, 44, 47, 49
Death, 18, 21, 19, 52, 57. *See* Transmigration
Divine Feminine, 2, 12, 16, 25, 32, 33, 38
Divine Love, 41, 42, 60, 76, 78
Divinity, 12, 14
Donkey, 1, 52, 74
Existential, 1, 18, 25, 42, 44, 47, 52, 66, 71, 74
Family, 12, 19, 25, 52, 66, 71
Fantasy, 5, 8, 32
Feminism, 16, 21. *See* Divine Feminine
Home, 18, 19, 25, 33, 38, 47, 60, 66
Israel, 9, 34
LGBTQ, 3, 5, 6, 8, 9, 8, 32, 33, 38, 42, 59, 62
Loneliness, 12
Loss, 9, 19, 33, 34, 64, 76
Love, 2, 31, 32, 38, 41, 60, 62, 72, 76, 78
Masturbation, 3, 5. *See* Fantasy
New York, 3, 31, 34, 42, 44, 47, 49
Nightlife, 3, 42
Past Life, 50, 74. *See* Transmigration
Rain, 6, 12, 25, 41, 50, 60, 78
Reality, 25, 44, 57, 66, 70
Sex, 5, 6, 8, 14, 42, 59
Skin, 12, 14, 71
Society, 12, 18, 19, 25, 66
Suburbs, 25, 66. *See* Existential
Time, 3, 18, 25, 32, 49, 66, 71
Thousand Eyes, 5, 33, 39, 63. *See* Divine Feminine
Transcendence, 12, 14, 18, 25, 38, 42, 47, 49, 50, 76, 78, 74
Transmigration, 14, 18, 50, 51, 57
Vietnam, 19

Facebook jistrangeway.official
Instagram jistrangeway
www.jistrangeway.com

ALSO BY JI STRANGEWAY

RED AS BLUE – GRAPHIC NOVEL

June Lusparian hovers on the edge of adulthood, searching Paradise High School for a hint of hope. She falls for Cheer Captain, Beverly, who awakens June's secret gift of music. As their nascent romance grows, they face a dark world on the verge of explosion.

NUNE – SHORT FILM

An offbeat teenage girl struggles for peer acceptance while vying for the unlikely love of an American beauty.

Nune is a modern, short film adaptation of *Red as Blue*, the novel. On iTunes, Google Play, Amazon and more!

SIGN UP FOR NEW RELEASES:
WWW.JISTRANGEWAY.COM/NEWS